Observing Children and Adolescents

Student Workbook

Observing Children and Adolescents

Student Workbook

Michie O. Swartwood, Ph.D.
SUNY, Cortland

Kathy H. Trotter, Ph.D.

THOMSON

WADSWORTH

Australia • Canada • Mexico • Singapore • Spain • United Kingdom • United States

Printed in the United States of America
5   6   7   07   06   05

Printer: Globus Printing

ISBN: 0-534-62272-0

For more information about our products,
contact us at:
Thomson Learning Academic Resource Center
1-800-423-0563

For permission to use material from this text,
contact us by:
Phone: 1-800-730-2214
Fax: 1-800-731-2215
Web: http://www.thomsonrights.com

Wadsworth/Thomson Learning
10 Davis Drive
Belmont, CA 94002-3098
USA

Asia
Thomson Learning
5 Shenton Way #01-01
UIC Building
Singapore 068808

Australia/New Zealand
Thomson Learning
102 Dodds Street
Southbank, Victoria 3006
Australia

Canada
Nelson
1120 Birchmount Road
Toronto, Ontario M1K 5G4
Canada

Europe/Middle East/South Africa
Thomson Learning
High Holborn House
50/51 Bedford Row
London WC1R 4LR
United Kingdom

Latin America
Thomson Learning
Seneca, 53
Colonia Polanco
11560 Mexico D.F.
Mexico

Spain/Portugal
Paraninfo
Calle/Magallanes, 25
28015 Madrid, Spain

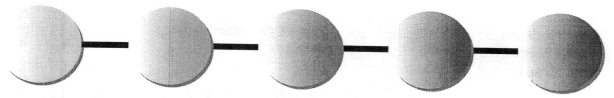

OBSERVING CHILDREN AND ADOLESCENTS

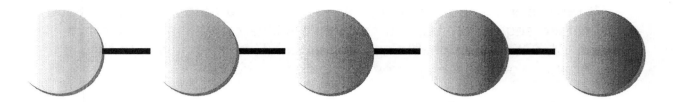

OBSERVING CHILDREN AND ADOLESCENTS WORKBOOK

INTRODUCTION: CONNECTING CONTENT

Welcome to *Observing Children and Adolescents*, an observation program designed to provide you with a new way to experience and learn critical concepts in the field of child development. The goal of this program is to enhance your understanding of the major concepts and milestones of development through video illustration designed to connect a variety of important course theories with concrete examples.

We will explore physical, cognitive, and social-emotional development in children from birth through adolescence. We will cover a wide range of topics specific to each of the major content areas, divided chronologically among an ethnically diverse population. The program is designed to allow you to see, not just read or hear about, real children achieving the milestones of development, interacting with each other and caregivers, and participating in classic experiments.

Through extended overviews and carefully directed questions, this workbook will provide you with the opportunity to review the narrated video content and connect it to the information that you are learning in class and from your text. The unnarrated observation modules allow you to apply your knowledge to real-life situations, using context-based examples that can be viewed from multiple perspectives. These less structured observational exercises more closely mirror the complexity encountered in observing the development of a child.

Each section of the workbook is divided into the following four sections:

Overview – The overview provides a brief summary of the narrated video segments. Important concepts illustrated in the video are outlined, with an emphasis on application. This overview sets the foundation for a review of key terms and concepts.

Key Terms and Concepts – This section covers concepts and terms which are relevant for the developmental changes illustrated in the video. Comprehensive definitions are provided for each term, helping you solidify your factual knowledge base.

Application: Knowledge in Action – This section of the workbook is designed to help you make important connections between key terms and concepts and real life situations. A series of open-ended questions are presented to stimulate critical thinking and to help you integrate and apply concepts illustrated in the video.

Observation Module: Research and Theories in Action – The observational video segments included for each module allow you to assess your ability to apply your knowledge. These video segments are unstructured and demonstrate a variety of developmental concepts. Observation module questions are designed to require you to integrate multiple perspectives, using information presented in class, in your text and workbook, and in the video.

OBSERVING CHILDREN AND ADOLESCENTS
0 TO 2 YEARS

PRENATAL ASSESSMENT

Dr. Cohen performs a detailed ultrasound on Eleanor Walsh who is in her 4th month of pregnancy. The ultrasound uses sound waves to produce an image of the unborn child for analysis. During a routine prenatal visit, ultrasound is used to estimate fetal age, determine the position and growth of the baby, and determine the health of the placenta. In high-risk pregnancies, the ultrasound is used to help rule out birth defects. Women approaching or beyond the age of 35 have a higher risk of having a baby with Down's syndrome and other chromosomal abnormalities. While the ultrasound cannot diagnose chromosomal or other abnormalities, it is a useful screen for estimating risk and the need for additional diagnostic tests such as amniocentesis.

KEY TERMS AND CONCEPTS

Amniocentesis: A prenatal assessment technique performed in the 11th to 14th week of pregnancy in which a needle is inserted into the mother's womb and a small amount of amniotic fluid is withdrawn and tested for genetic defects.

Chorionic villus sampling (CVS): A procedure used to diagnose birth defects in the first trimester of pregnancy that involves inserting a thin tube through the vagina and cervix or a needle through the mother's abdomen to collect a sample of fetal cells from the chorion membrane surrounding the fetus.

Chromosomal abnormalities: A problem with the chromosomes, either inherited or due to mutations, that leads to birth defects.

Down's syndrome: A genetic condition caused by an extra chromosome 21.

High-risk pregnancy: A pregnancy is considered high risk if the mother is over the age of 35 or has experienced a previous pregnancy with a birth defect, if there is a family history of genetic or birth defects, and if the results of other screening tests are abnormal.

Placenta: An organ that develops in the uterus just days after conception that provides respiration and nourishment for the unborn child and takes away waste.

Spina Bifida: A birth defect in which the spine fails to close properly.

Ultrasound: A prenatal assessment technique that uses sound waves to produce an image of the unborn child to estimate fetal age, to determine the position and growth of the baby, and to determine the health of the placenta.

0 to 2
**Prenatal Development, Birth
and the Newborn**
Prenatal Assessment

Name _____
Section _____

APPLICATION: KNOWLEDGE IN ACTION

1. According to Dr. Cohen, what is the most common chromosomal abnormality seen in live-born babies? What is the prevalence of this disorder? What is the relationship between maternal age and the risk of having a baby with this disorder?

2. Dr. Cohen explains how multiple prenatal assessment measures can be used together to make decisions regarding whether further medical monitoring procedures, such as amniocentesis, are necessary. Does he recommend an amniocentesis for Eleanor? Why or why not?

0 to 2
Prenatal Development, Birth
and the Newborn
Prenatal Assessment

Name _____

Section _____

3. Describe the ultrasound procedure as performed by Dr. Cohen. What is the position of the baby? What structures does Dr. Cohen identify? What important health information is learned as a result of this ultrasound test? Be specific.

4. Describe two structural abnormalities and/or markers of chromosomal abnormalities discussed by Dr. Cohen as he performs the ultrasound.

5. What risks are associated with various prenatal assessment measures? How are decisions made regarding which measures to use? What are some ethical considerations in the use of prenatal monitoring procedures?

6. How prevalent are birth defects resulting from genetic factors? How can the family histories of prospective parents be used to determine the likelihood of a baby having a genetic disorder?

0 to 2
**Prenatal Development, Birth
and the Newborn**
Prenatal Assessment

Name _____

Section _____

7. What are some other, non-genetic factors that can affect prenatal development? Are there certain time periods in pregnancy when the developing baby is more vulnerable than others? Why?

8. Eleanor began taking prenatal vitamins 3 months prior to conception, and she stopped consuming alcohol in the month prior to conception. What problems will her careful, planned approach likely rule out? What other behaviors may affect the health of a child prior to, or very early in, pregnancy?

Birth

About to give birth, this mother is well into the second stage of labor – pushing and delivery of the baby. Contractions have become longer, stronger, and more frequent. This stage of labor, which lasts approximately one hour, is shorter than the first stage, which may take from 12 to 14 hours or longer in first pregnancies. In the final stage of labor, mild contractions lead to separation and delivery of the placenta, the baby's life support system while inside the womb.

Weighing in at 8 pounds and 19 inches long, bow-legged, wrinkled, red, screaming, and covered in vernix, Carter represents the typical newborn. The APGAR test is used to quickly assess this newborn's overall physical condition. Newborns are rated at one minute and five minutes after delivery on five distinct qualities: appearance, pulse, grimace, activity, and respiration. For each category, the minimum score is 0, the maximum score is 2. The baby's scores for each of the five categories are added together to get the final APGAR score.

KEY TERMS AND CONCEPTS

1st stage of labor: Begins with regular contractions and dilation and thinning of the cervix and ends when the cervix is fully dilated.

2nd stage of labor: Pushing and delivery of the baby.

3rd stage of labor: Separation and delivery of the placenta.

Alternative birth center: An alternative to the traditional hospital maternity environment that offers a home-like setting for labor and delivery.

APGAR test: An assessment technique performed at one minute and at five minutes after birth to estimate the newborn's overall physical condition.

Lamaze: An approach to childbirth that emphasizes drug-free labor and delivery and teaches relaxation, breathing, and imagery techniques to ease the pain.

Natural or prepared childbirth: Labor and delivery that is free of medical intervention.

Vernix: A white substance that covers and protects the baby's skin in utero.

APPLICATION: KNOWLEDGE IN ACTION

1. In the video, Lee has her baby in a hospital setting, without fetal monitoring or anesthesia. What are some other approaches to childbirth outlined in your text? How might a high-risk pregnancy impact birthing choices?

2. Lee was in labor for 9 hours with her first child, Carter. Is this typical? If she has other children, is her labor experience likely to be similar or different? Why?

0 to 2
**Prenatal Development, Birth
and the Newborn**
Birth

Name _____
Section _____

3. Lee and Dan were worried about the size of Carter's testicles and his somewhat flattened facial features. Discuss the newborn baby's appearance and explain the likely duration of these characteristics.

4. What does the acronym APGAR stand for?

0 to 2
Prenatal Development, Birth
and the Newborn
Birth

Name _____

Section _____

5. How are each of the five areas tested by the APGAR rated? Explain the APGAR score ratings in connection with good, fair, and poor condition.

6. What was Carter's APGAR score? Describe, in detail, how Dr. Shapiro arrived at this score.

0 to 2
**Prenatal Development, Birth
and the Newborn**
Birth

Name _____
Section _____

7. Why is this test performed twice, at one minute and at five minutes after birth?

8. Does the APGAR score predict the future health of a baby?

THE NEWBORN: SENSATION AND PERCEPTION

At birth, infants are well equipped to face the world. In fact, many of the baby's sensory capabilities are well developed *before* birth. Hearing develops pre-natally, and, at birth, newborns show a preference for familiar voices such as mom's or dad's. They will orient to new sounds and are especially sensitive to high-pitched tones.

Vision is the least mature of the newborn's sensory capacities. At birth, infants can see clearly only at distances between 8 and 12 inches. They are very nearsighted, but their vision is ideally suited for gazing into the face of a caregiver while being fed or held. When held closely, they will fixate on a face and imitate facial expressions and can follow a moving object with their eyes. Infants have clear visual preferences – they will gaze longer at bold patterns with strong contrast and when given the choice of other interesting alternatives, prefer to look at the human face.

KEY TERMS AND CONCEPTS

Hearing: Hearing develops pre-natally, and, at birth, newborns show a preference for familiar voices such as mom's or dad's; they will orient to new sounds and are especially sensitive to high-pitched tones.

Vision: The least developed of the newborn's sensory capacities; at birth, infants are very nearsighted and can see clearly only at distances between 8 and 12 inches.

Visual preferences: Infants show clear visual preferences; they will gaze longer at bold patterns with strong contrast, and when given the choice of other interesting alternatives, prefer to look at the human face.

APPLICATION: KNOWLEDGE IN ACTION

1. What does research tell us about the sensory capacities of newborns, such as Carter and Aiden? Cite evidence from the video that supports this research in regard to vision and hearing.

2. Discuss how the newborn's capacities for vision and hearing are adaptive in the context of Carter's initial interaction with mom.

0 to 2

**Prenatal Development, Birth
and the Newborn**
The Newborn: Sensation and Perception

Name _____

Section _____

3. Infants have clear visual preferences. Discuss the visual preferences of infants in the context of the response of 2-month-old Giuseppina to the stimuli presented by Dr. Basow. What method is Dr. Basow using as a test of Giuseppina's visual preferences? What other methods are commonly used to study infant sensory and perceptual capacities?

4. Does the newborn's preference for looking at faces more than at other objects indicate that form perception is innate? Why or why not?

THE NEWBORN: REFLEX DEVELOPMENT

Reflexes are innate or unlearned, automatic responses that allow newborns to respond to their environment. Many reflexes, breathing, swallowing, and sucking for example, have survival value. Other, more primitive reflexes, like the Moro and grasping, are considered leftovers from our evolutionary heritage. Survival reflexes usually become voluntary at some point during the first year, while the primitive reflexes disappear. Absence, persistence beyond the normal time for disappearance, or the reappearance of a reflex later in life is suggestive of significant neurological problems.

KEY TERMS AND CONCEPTS

Babinski reflex: A reflex elicited by stroking the bottom of an infant's foot that causes the big toe to flex towards the top of the foot and the other toes to fan out.

Moro reflex: A reflex seen in response to loud noise or sudden movement in which the infant throws back his head, extends his arms and legs, then quickly brings them back in towards his body as if to hold on to something.

Palmar grasping reflex: A reflex seen in response to tactile stimulation or stroking of the palm in which the infant closes his hands and fingers in a grasp.

Primitive reflexes: Inborn responses that disappear at some point during the first year.

Reflex: Genetically preprogrammed responses to certain stimuli.

Rooting reflex: A reflex seen in response to tactile stimulation or stroking of the cheek in which the infant turns his head in the direction of the stroking.

Stepping reflex: When held upright with feet touching a flat surface, infants appear to take steps and walk.

Sucking reflex: Stimulation of the mouth causes the infant to suck automatically.

Survival reflexes: Inborn responses such as sucking and swallowing that become voluntary at some point during the first year.

APPLICATION: KNOWLEDGE IN ACTION

1. What is a reflex? Using specific examples from the video, discuss the difference between primitive and survival reflexes. How are survival reflexes adaptive for the infant?

2. One-week-old Aiden exhibits two reflexes that are related to the nourishment of the infant. Describe the reflexes exhibited by Aiden. What is the developmental course of each of these reflexes?

3. Mackenzie and Aiden both exhibit reflexes that are thought to be related to the protection of the infant. Describe the reflexes exhibited by Mackenzie and Aiden. What is the developmental course of each of these reflexes?

4. Olivia, who is 2½ weeks old, exhibits the stepping reflex. How does Dr. Basow elicit this reflex in Olivia? What possible purpose does this reflex serve? Is the stepping reflex indicative of a walking instinct? Why or why not?

5. At approximately what age will the following reflexes disappear: grasping, Babinski, Moro, Palmar, rooting, stepping, sucking? Will they be replaced by voluntary behavior? Why or why not?

6. What important diagnostic purpose do reflexes serve? Specifically, what is indicated by the absence or persistence of primitive reflexes beyond the normal time for disappearance? Cite two examples from the video in your answer.

INFANTS AND TODDLERS: SENSATION AND PERCEPTION

SMELL, TASTE, AND VISION

Infants are highly sensitive to odors. They turn towards pleasant odors, such as vanilla, and will make faces of disgust and turn away from unpleasant odors, such as rotten eggs. Their sense of taste is also well developed. Changes in facial expression and rates of sucking indicate that infants can distinguish between the four basic tastes – sweet, sour, salty, and bitter.

At birth, visual acuity is estimated to be about 20/600, which means that the newborn is able to see at 20 feet what an adult with normal visual acuity can see clearly from a distance of 600 feet. Visual acuity improves rapidly, however, reaching 20/100 by 6 months and approximating adult vision by 1 year of age. At 2 to 3 months of age, all basic colors can be discerned and tracking of moving objects is at the adult level.

As infants continue to improve in their visual capacities, they show evidence of perceptions regarding depth and distance. The visual cliff is an apparatus used by researchers to study the visual perceptual abilities of infants. The "cliff" consists of a glass table-top with a checkered pattern positioned close to the glass on one side, the shallow side, and far below the glass on the other side to give the appearance of depth. Infants as young as six months avoid the cliff, and even when coaxed by a parent, refuse to cross to the deep side of the table.

KEY TERMS AND CONCEPTS

Depth perception: The ability to see in three dimensions and judge distances.

Smell: Infants are highly sensitive to odors. They turn towards pleasant odors, such as vanilla, and will make faces of disgust and turn away from unpleasant odors, such as rotten eggs.

Taste: Infants can distinguish 4 basic tastes: sweet, sour, salty, and bitter; Sweet tastes are preferred and appear to have a soothing effect.

Vision: At birth, visual acuity is estimated to be between 20/400 and 20/600 but improves rapidly, reaching 20/100 by 6 months and approximating adult vision by 1 year of age. At 2 to 3 months of age, all basic colors can be discerned and tracking of moving objects is at the adult level.

Visual cliff: An apparatus used to study infant depth perception that consists of a tabletop that is half opaque and half transparent, giving the appearance of a drop off or cliff on one side.

0 to 2
Infants and Toddlers – Sensation,
Perception, and Motor Development
Infants and Toddlers – Smell, Taste, and Vision

Name _____

Section _____

APPLICATION: KNOWLEDGE IN ACTION

1. Research suggests that infants are born with very definite smell and taste preferences. Do the responses of 6-week-old Aislynne and 4-month-old Delaney support these research findings? Why or why not?

2. How might taste and smell preferences impact infant behavior? How are these preferences adaptive for the infant?

0 to 2

Infants and Toddlers – Sensation,
Perception, and Motor Development
Infants and Toddlers – Smell, Taste, and Vision

Name _____

Section _____

3. Describe the differences between 1-week-old Aiden, 2-month-old Giuseppina, and 9-month-old Hannah in their abilities to visually track a moving object. How do sensory and motor skills interact to promote this ability?

4. How do 9-month-old Elizabeth and 11-month-old Nicholas respond when they are placed beside the visual cliff? Is their response consistent with the research on depth perception? Why or why not?

0 to 2

Infants and Toddlers – Sensation,
Perception, and Motor Development
Infants and Toddlers – Smell, Taste, and Vision

Name _____

Section _____

5. Discuss the relationship between motor development, independent movement, and depth perception. Why do Elizabeth and Nicholas respond the way they do?

6. What methods do researchers use to determine whether or not children who are too young to crawl are able to perceive depth? What do their studies tell us?

INFANTS AND TODDLERS: MOTOR DEVELOPMENT

GROSS MOTOR DEVELOPMENT

Early motor development follows the cephalocaudal and proximodistal principles; that is, development proceeds from the head down and from the middle of the body to the outer parts of the body. Infants first gain control over their neck muscles, allowing them to lift their heads while lying on their stomach. Next, they begin to develop shoulder and chest control, which allows them to elevate their chest and head using their arms. Trunk control follows, and later, rolling and sitting with support becomes possible.

Once an infant has gained voluntary control over the upper and middle parts of the body, development of the extremities quickly follows. Soon, the infant is crawling, pulling-up to a standing position, and walking using furniture for support. At about one year of age, children typically begin walking alone. Although there is wide individual variation in the exact ages at which infants acquire specific gross motor skills, they progress through the same sequence of motor achievements fairly consistently.

KEY TERMS AND CONCEPTS

Cephalocaudal trend: Physical maturation and growth that proceeds from head to toe.

Dynamic systems theory: The view that motor development involves a complex system of actions rather than the development of independent skills.

Experiential or practice hypothesis: The view that experience and practice are critical for the development of locomotor skills.

Gross motor skills: Skills involving large muscle movements or movements of the entire body.

Maturational viewpoint: The view that motor skills develop in a genetically pre-programmed sequence.

Proximodistal trend: Physical maturation and growth that proceeds from the center of the body to the extremities.

APPLICATION: KNOWLEDGE IN ACTION

1. Describe differences in the gross motor development of Giuseppina, Anthony, Hannah, Holly, and Steven. How do these differences illustrate the cephalocaudal and proximodistal principles?

2. Outline developmental milestones for acquisition of the following gross motor skills: lifting head, elevating chest, rolling over, sitting with support, sitting without support, pulling-up to a stand, standing alone, walking with support, walking alone.

3. Hannah and Holly are both 9 months old, yet their gross motor skills are not equally developed. Discuss individual variations in gross motor development. Are Hannah and Holly both developing typically? Will Hannah and Holly likely develop gross motor skills in the same sequence? Why or why not?

4. Discuss 3 possible explanations for the sequencing and timing of early motor development. Cite examples from the video that lend support to each of these viewpoints.

FINE MOTOR DEVELOPMENT

Infants continue to gain control of their hands and fingers throughout infancy and toddlerhood. While the Palmar grasping reflex is present at birth, voluntary grasping develops later. Infants develop their grasping skills in a particular sequence, first using an ulnar grasp, whereby an object is grasped by placing the finger against the palm of the hand. Later, they develop a pincer grasp, using the thumb and forefinger to grasp an object. An infant's developing fine motor skills allow her to interact with her environment in new ways, such as building towers and using a pen to make marks on paper. As infants develop, they gain not only more control of their fine motor movements, but also the ability to better coordinate their motor skills.

KEY TERMS AND CONCEPTS

Fine motor skills: Skills involving fine body movements, like movements of the hands and fingers.

Pincer grasp: Use of the thumb and forefinger to pick up or explore an object.

Pre-reaching: Uncoordinated swipes and swings.

Ulnar grasp: Grasping an object by pressing fingers against the palm of the hand.

0 to 2
Infants and Toddlers – Sensation,
Perception, and Motor Development
Infants and Toddlers – Fine Motor

Name _____

Section _____

APPLICATION: KNOWLEDGE IN ACTION

1. At what age does voluntary reaching typically emerge? Describe the development of voluntary reaching and grasping, including the milestones of voluntary reaching and the average age at which each skill is attained. Which infants presented in the video illustrate each of these milestones?

2. Hannah and Elizabeth are both 9 months old, yet their grasping skills differ. Is Hannah's fine motor development more or less advanced than Elizabeth's? Is Hannah's or Elizabeth's development atypical? Why or why not?

3. Using specific examples from the video, discuss how increases in finger control and manipulatory skills impact the developing child's interactions in the environment.

INFANTS AND TODDLERS: COGNITIVE DEVELOPMENT

EARLY LEARNING

Newborn babies may appear to be passively watching the world go by, but studies show that their perceptions produce changes in behavior – changes that can't be explained by heredity or maturation. This means that learning is occurring, a process that can be shown even when an infant is just a few hours old. Newborns are able to imitate a number of adult facial gestures, and while there is some debate about whether they are processing information about facial expression, it is clear that they are perceiving and reproducing something in the environment.

One form of early learning, habituation, is easily observed. An infant is presented with a toy, which initially interests him. The toy is presented until he habituates or becomes disinterested and stops responding to the toy. When a new or novel toy is presented, he dishabituates, or responds to, the novel stimulus, indicating that he notices something different.

KEY TERMS AND CONCEPTS

Classical conditioning: Learning based on associations between a stimulus and a response.

Dishabituation: An increase in response that occurs when a new or novel stimulus is presented.

Habituation: A decline in response to a repeated stimulus.

Learning: A change in behavior that results from experience.

Observational learning: Learning through observation and imitation.

Operant conditioning: A form of learning based on consequences.

APPLICATION: KNOWLEDGE IN ACTION

1. Outline methodologies used to study learning in early infancy. How can researchers determine whether or not a newborn or young infant "remembers" something?

2. One-week-old Aiden and 9-month-old Holly both reproduce behaviors exhibited by their mothers. Describe their behavior. Discuss the relative roles of maturation and learning in Aiden's and Holly's imitative behavior.

3. Six-week-old Aislynne's behavior illustrates a form of learning called habituation. Describe her behavior and discuss how it provides evidence for learning in early infancy.

PIAGET'S SENSORIMOTOR STAGE

Jean Piaget proposed a comprehensive theory of child cognitive development, identifying four major periods, or stages, of cognitive development. The first of these stages, the sensorimotor stage spans the age range from birth to two years. During the sensorimotor stage, infants learn to coordinate sensory information and motor activity, becoming increasingly able to act purposefully on their environments and solve problems.

At the beginning of the sensorimotor period, an infant's actions are confined to innate reflexes like sucking and grasping. Soon, however, an infant will begin to show what Piaget called primary circular reactions. Primary circular reactions involve simple, repetitive acts centered on an infant's own body. Later, infants begin to show secondary circular reactions; that is, they make interesting things happen in the world outside their own bodies. They also begin to show coordination of secondary schemes, using two or more previously acquired schemes to achieve a goal. Finally, infants develop tertiary circular reactions; that is, they begin to actively experiment with the world.

Children also develop the ability to represent objects mentally by the end of the sensorimotor period – this is an important cognitive change, as it allows children to think about things that they can't see or touch. As children approach the age of two, they begin to have the ability to solve problems using insight and mental experimentation, as opposed to relying exclusively on trial and error.

The development of object permanence is one of the more notable cognitive changes occurring during the sensorimotor period. Very young infants are unaware that objects continue to exist when they are no longer visible. As they develop object permanence, they begin to retrieve objects that are partially hidden behind a barrier, eventually reaching behind a barrier to retrieve an object that is completely hidden.

KEY TERMS AND CONCEPTS

Cognitive development: The development of cognitive processes such as thinking, knowing, and remembering.

Coordination of secondary schemes: Infants use two or more previously acquired schemes to achieve a goal.

Invariant developmental sequence: Development proceeds in a particular sequence or order.

Object permanence: The knowledge that objects exist independent of one's perception or action on them.

Primary circular reaction: Simple, repetitive acts centered on the infant's own body.

Reflex activity: Actions are confined to innate reflexes such as sucking or grasping.

Scheme: A pattern of thought or action that one constructs to organize information about the world.

Secondary circular reaction: Simple, repetitive acts that are centered on an external object.

Sensorimotor stage: The cognitive stage in which infants coordinate sensory input and motor capabilities, forming behavioral schemes that permit them to get to know and act on their environments.

Symbolic problem solving: Infants can solve problems without the necessity of trial and error; they can experiment mentally.

Tertiary circular reactions: Infants discover new methods of solving problems or producing interesting results through active experimentation.

APPLICATION: KNOWLEDGE IN ACTION

1. Describe Jean Piaget's sensorimotor period of cognitive development. How do sensory and motor activities interact in the development of cognitive skills, according to Piaget?

2. Describe the behaviors of 1-week-old Aiden and 2-month-old Giuseppina. Are their behaviors purposeful? Discuss differences in their behaviors with regard to Piaget's concept of the circular reaction.

3. Describe the behaviors of 6-week-old Aislynne and 5-month-old James. Do their behaviors illustrate primary or secondary circular reactions? Why?

4. Which infant presented in the video illustrates Piaget's concept of the coordination of secondary schemes? Describe the infant's behavior. How old is the infant?

5. Which infant illustrates a tertiary circular reaction? Describe the infant's behavior. Approximately how old is this infant?

6. Outline the development of object permanence by describing the behaviors of 2-month-old Giuseppina, 6-month-old Anthony, and 20-month-old Tess with respect to hidden objects. What do their behaviors indicate regarding their mental representation abilities? Which of them has developed object permanence?

INFANTS AND TODDLERS: LANGUAGE DEVELOPMENT

Language is both receptive and expressive – it involves both listening to and understanding others in communicating needs, wants, and desires. At all ages, gains in expressive language are far outweighed by gains in receptive language. Infants are highly responsive to language – they smile, vocalize when spoken to, make vowel-like intonations called cooing, and turn in the direction of voices and sounds.

Caregivers typically have a higher pitched speech style, with wider fluctuations in intonation, called motherese or parentese, when speaking to infants. This is seen worldwide and is believed to not only attract an infant's attention, but also to cause him to focus on certain patterns in language.

An early expressive language milestone occurs when an infant begins babbling, or repeating consonant-vowel combinations such as "ma ma ma" and "da da da."

Even before children begin to use words, they use gestures, such as reaching for an object to express their desires. The also learn a variety of language functions from joint activities with caregivers, such as reading picture books. Naming, turn-taking, and question and answer interactions are developed through these activities.

At about one year, most children say their first recognizable words. Gestures continue to serve an important communication function for infants, however. They soon learn that pointing, reaching, or other forms of nonverbal communication in conjunction with language will often lead to the desired result more quickly.

Toward the end of the first year, children begin to use telegraphic, or telegram-like, speech, combining words into simple sentences in which only the words that are absolutely necessary to communicate an idea are used.

Children develop expressive language in the context of interactions with adults, who continue to use child-directed speech, often expanding or enriching the child's ungrammatical speech and modeling both appropriate speech and increases in length and complexity of sentences. This sets the stage for the dramatic increases in vocabulary and syntactic complexity seen in early childhood.

KEY TERMS AND CONCEPTS

Babbling: The production of consonant-vowel combinations such as "pa" and "ba"; peaks between 9 and 12 months of age.

Child-directed speech: Short, simple sentences with a high-pitched tone and an emphasis on key words.

Cooing: The production of vowel-like sounds typical at about 2 months of age.

Expansion: Repetition of grammatically incorrect speech in a grammatically correct fashion that may include some elaboration.

Expressive language: Language production.

First words: Typically at about 1 year of age; a shift from playing with sounds to planned, controlled speech.

Holophrase: The use of one word to express an idea behind an entire phrase.

Joint activities: Activities between a caregiver and a child, such as pat-a-cake, peek-a-boo, and reading a favorite picture book, that imitate the turn-taking pattern of speech and highlight the meaning and function of spoken words.

Nonverbal communication: Pointing, gestures, facial expressions; typically appears around 8 to 10 months of age and is used to influence the behavior of others.

Recast: A form of rephrasing a child's speech in which new elements or grammatical forms are added.

Receptive language: Language comprehension.

Telegraphic speech: Typically at 18 to 24 months of age; simple noun-verb combinations used to communicate an idea.

0 to 2
**Infants and Toddlers – Cognitive and
Language Development, Social and
Emotional Development**
Language Development

Name _____

Section _____

APPLICATION: KNOWLEDGE IN ACTION

1. Research shows that infants are responsive to language from the day they are born. How do infants respond to language behaviorally? Give examples from the video that illustrate the infant's behavioral responses to language.

2. Using specific examples from the video, outline the milestones of language development during the first two years.

3. Discuss the importance of environmental supports for language development. Provide examples from the video that illustrate environmental supports, including child-directed speech, joint activities, expansion, and recasts.

4. Discuss the role of gestures and other nonverbal responses that often accompany children's vocal communication. Cite at least three examples from the video that illustrate the importance of nonverbal communication.

0 to 2
**Infants and Toddlers – Cognitive and
Language Development, Social and
Emotional Development**
Language Development

Name _____

Section _____

5. What is the difference between expressive and receptive language?
   Which develops first, expressive or receptive language? Cite specific
   examples from the video to support your answer.

INFANTS AND TODDLERS: SOCIAL AND EMOTIONAL DEVELOPMENT

TEMPERAMENT

At birth, babies appear to have unique temperaments, or characteristic patterns of responding in the world. These temperamental patterns are believed to be biologically based, and they strongly influence the interactions that babies have with their caregivers. Researchers have grouped these temperamental patterns into three broad categories: some babies are easy, some are difficult, and some are slow-to-warm-up.

Easy babies exhibit a generally positive mood. They are easily comforted, eat and sleep on a regular schedule, and readily adapt to new situations. Difficult babies are more negative in mood, and they do not tolerate discomfort, such as hunger, well at all. They are irregular in their eating and sleeping schedules, and can be very hard to comfort when upset. Slow-to-warm-up babies are moody and slower to adapt to change. They are often characterized as fussy, showing more negativity in mood than easy babies, but eventually warming up as caregivers persist with attempts to comfort them.

KEY TERMS AND CONCEPTS

Difficult temperament: The difficult baby is active, generally negative in mood, has unpredictable, irregular habits, and adapts slowly to new people or situations.

Easy temperament: The easy baby is generally positive in mood, adapts quickly to new situations, and has regular, predictable habits.

Goodness of fit: A match or "fit" between the child's temperament and the child-rearing environment, resulting in secure attachment regardless of temperamental style.

Slow-to-warm-up temperament: The slow-to-warm-up baby is inactive, somewhat negative in mood, has variable habits, and adapts slowly to new situations.

Temperament: Typical way of responding emotionally and behaviorally to the environment.

0 to 2
Infants and Toddlers – Cognitive and Language Development, Social and Emotional Development
Social and Emotional Development – Temperament

Name _____

Section _____

APPLICATION: KNOWLEDGE IN ACTION

1. Discuss the temperament construct. How is temperament measured? What behaviors are studied in temperament research and why?

2. Behavioral dimensions of temperament tend to cluster into 3 broad temperamental profiles. Based on the description of 4-month-old Abby's behavior given by her caregiver, how would you characterize her temperament? Describe specific aspects of Abby's temperament that support your conclusion.

0 to 2

Infants and Toddlers – Cognitive and Language Development, Social and Emotional Development
Social and Emotional Development – Temperament

Name _____

Section _____

3. Describe two additional temperamental profiles. Use examples from the video to illustrate the typical characteristics of children who fit these profiles.

ATTACHMENT

Attachment is a strong, enduring bond that develops between a child and his or her caregiver. Attachment forms through a reciprocal relationship between a caregiver and an infant. Over time, if a caregiver is sensitive and responsive to an infant's needs and cues, the caregiver and infant will likely develop synchrony, or reciprocal, cooperative interactions that help build strong attachments.

Very young infants are responsive to human contact in general, responding to and accepting the comfort of a stranger. Over time, however, they begin to show a strong preference, or a specific attachment, for the people who care for them the most. As specific attachments develop, infants begin to show both a fear of strangers and separation anxiety. They will show distress when they are approached by a stranger or separated from their primary caregiver. As children and parents interact over time, separation anxiety decreases. Children begin to understand that separations are temporary, and they are comforted by a variety of familiar caregivers.

KEY TERMS AND CONCEPTS

Asocial phase: Infants from birth to 6 weeks show indiscriminate responsiveness to a variety of stimuli.

Attachment: The strong bond between a child and his or her caregiver.

Phase of indiscriminate attachments: Infants between 6 weeks to 6 to 8 months of age show a preference for human company in general.

Phase of multiple attachments: By 18 months of age infants have become attached to multiple caregivers.

Phase of specific attachment: Infants between 7 and 9 months show intense attachment to a specific caregiver and active proximity-seeking behaviors.

Secure base phenomenon: The child uses the caregiver as a secure base from which to explore the environment, returning from time to time for emotional refueling.

Separation anxiety: Distress exhibited by an infant when separated from the primary caregiver.

Stranger anxiety: Distress exhibited by an infant when approached by a stranger.

Synchrony: The cooperative, reciprocal interaction between a caregiver and child.

APPLICATION: KNOWLEDGE IN ACTION

1. What is an emotional attachment? Using the interaction between Aislynne and her mother to illustrate, discuss the reciprocal nature of parent-infant attachments.

2. Describe how emotional attachments develop. Include specific examples from the video that illustrate the concepts of stranger anxiety and separation anxiety in the study of attachment.

0 to 2
Infants and Toddlers – Cognitive and Language Development, Social and Emotional Development
Social and Emotional Development – Attachment

Name _____

Section _____

3. How is the security of attachment measured? Describe 9-month-old Olivia's behavior when her mother leaves the room, as well as when she returns. How would you describe the quality of Olivia's attachment? Why? Why do we need to know how she behaves upon her mother's return?

4. Describe how Olivia would have reacted to her mother's departure and return for each of the following attachment patterns: secure, resistant, avoidant, and disorganized/disoriented.

GENDER

Most would agree that boys and girls, from a very early age, play and act differently from each other. Although research shows that there are very early sex differences in behavior, these differences are small and accentuated by environmental influences. Adults describe newborn boys and girls very differently–even when there are no differences in size or weight. Boys are described as stronger, more active, and independent, and girls as more delicate, passive, and dependent.

Even the physical environment reinforces sex-typed behavior. Girls are more often dressed in pink and boys in blue. More masculine toys are chosen for boys and more feminine toys for girls, and children's bedrooms often reflect gender-specific themes. By the age of 2, children show a preference for same-sex playmates and are more likely to engage in gender-specific play activities.

KEY TERMS AND CONCEPTS

Expressive role: A role typically encouraged in females that involves being kind, nurturant, cooperative, and sensitive to the needs of others.

Gender role: Society's expectations for appropriate masculine or feminine behavior.

Gender segregation: Children's tendency to show a preference for same-sex playmates.

Gender-typed behavior: Children's tendency to engage in gender appropriate activities and play with gender-appropriate toys.

Gender typing: How children acquire their ideas of gender appropriate behaviors and preferences.

Instrumental role: A role typically encouraged in males that involves being dominant, assertive, independent, and competitive.

0 to 2

Infants and Toddlers – Cognitive and Language Development, Social and Emotional Development
Social and Emotional Development – Gender

Name _____

Section _____

APPLICATION: KNOWLEDGE IN ACTION

1. Are sex differences present at birth or learned? Support your answer with research. What evidence can you find in the video to support the idea that they are present at birth or learned?

2. How do the adults in the video describe their children in terms of gender? How do parental expectations contribute to children's ideas of gender-appropriate roles and activities?

0 to 2
Infants and Toddlers – Cognitive and Language Development, Social and Emotional Development
Social and Emotional Development – Gender

Name _____

Section _____

3. In what ways does the physical environment reinforce gender role stereotypes and gender-typed behavior? Give examples from the video.

4. At what age do children begin to engage in gender-specific play? Describe the play interactions illustrated on the video. Are these children engaged in gender specific play activities? Do they learn to choose these play activities, or are they biologically based? Why?

CONNECTING CONTENT: RESEARCH AND THEORIES IN ACTION

Summary of Observation Module Content

- Aislynne, 6 weeks old, interacting with mom.
- James, 5 months, Olivia, 9 months, and Hayden, 9 months.
- Hayden, 9 months, and mom reading a book.
- Tess, 20 months.

Observation Module Questions	**Name** _____
0 to 2 Years	**Section** _____

1. John Bowlby's ethological theory of attachment is a widely accepted view of the development of attachment between a child and his or her caregiver. Discuss the attachment construct from the perspective of Bowlby's ethological theory. If John Bowlby were to observe the interaction between Aislynne and her mother, what characteristics of the interaction would he cite to support his theory?

2. Mary Ainsworth is well known for her research on infant attachment styles. What are the characteristics of a secure attachment pattern? What are the characteristics of the three patterns of insecurity identified by Ainsworth and her colleagues? What factors influence attachment security? How is attachment related to characteristics of the infant, including the temperament of the infant? How is attachment related to the quality of caregiving? Based on your observation of Aislynne's behavior and her mother's response, do you expect Aislynne's eventual attachment pattern to reflect a secure or insecure attachment? Why?

3. The dynamic systems perspective views development as a complex system of actions. Each new skill acquired is due to a combination of physical and cognitive maturation, environmental supports, and the goals of the infant. Describe the fine and gross motor achievements of the infants in this segment. Describe the cognitive achievements of the infants in this segment. How do the infants' physical abilities, cognitive maturation, and supports in the environment form an integrated system that leads to mastery of new skills? What role does the goals of the infant play?

4. Central to Jean Piaget's theory of cognitive development is the idea that children are active learners, constructing their own knowledge. As infants progress through the sensorimotor period, they move from depending on actual experiences with the world toward internal representation and the use of symbolic thought. Using specific examples from the video, discuss Piaget's view of cognitive development. How would the cognitive achievements of these infants be explained from Vygotsky's sociocultural viewpoint that emphasizes the role of social mediation in cognitive growth? How would information-processing theorists explain these changes?

5. Describe the language milestones achieved by each of the infants in the video. Do these specific examples support the learning/empiricist view that adults shape children's language acquisition by exhibiting and reinforcing correct grammatical speech or the nativist perspective that children are biologically predisposed to acquire language? Describe the social interactions between the infants in the video and others that support an interactionist perspective.

6. According to Erikson, toddlers are experiencing the psychosocial conflict he termed autonomy versus shame and doubt. How does the behavior of 20-month-old Tess illustrate this stage of psychosocial development? Based on the responses of Tess's mother to her behavior, do you expect Tess to successfully navigate this stage of development? Why or why not?

7. Twenty-month-old Tess is engaged in symbolic or "pretend play". Describe the play behavior of Tess. What does the play behavior of 20-month-old Tess tell you about her current level of cognitive development?

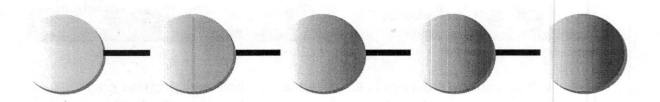

OBSERVING CHILDREN AND ADOLESCENTS
2 TO 5 YEARS

GROSS AND FINE MOTOR DEVELOPMENT

In early childhood, growth rates slow, with the average child growing 2 ½ inches in height and gaining 5 to 7 pounds a year. During this period, rapid gains are seen in gross motor skills, skills involving large muscle movements or movements of the entire body. At 3-years-of-age children can walk up and down stairs without assistance, walk or run in a straight line, and jump using both feet. By the age of four most children can hop on one foot, skip, and catch and throw a ball with some facility. They are also able to run faster and jump higher than they could at the age of 3, partly due to increased size, but also due to increased coordination of motor skills. Many 5-year-olds are able to ride a bicycle, effectively coordinating motor movements, visual information, and balance.

Between the ages of 2 and 5, children also improve dramatically in their ability to control and coordinate fine motor activity – skills that involve fine body movements, like the hands and fingers. As children gain more control over the muscles in their fingers, hands, and wrists, and as hand-eye coordination improves, they can manipulate puzzle pieces more easily. By the age of 3 or 4, most children have graduated from simple puzzles designed for ease of handling, to more complex ones. By 4 or 5, children are able to cut, draw, paint, and write. While their skills are clearly still developing, they are laying the foundation for the handwriting that they will practice in school.

KEY TERMS AND CONCEPTS

Catching: Progresses from catching with arms rigidly extended, to catching against the body with arms flexed, to catching with hands and fingers.

Climbing: At age 3, child ascends and descends stairs without alternating feet; by 4, is using alternate foot pattern; and by 5, efficiently climbing trees, ropes, and ladders.

Drawing and writing: Progresses from scribbling, to copying simple designs, to recognizable and meaningful representations of objects.

Jumping: Height and distance steadily increases from age 2 to 5.

Running: Control over stops, starts, and turns as well as speed increases steadily from age 2 to 5.

Self-help skills: Skills such as tying, buttoning, zipping, and using utensils that allow the preschooler more independence.

Skipping: The skipping of 3 and 4 year olds is typically a shuffling, one-footed skip; by 5, children are skipping using an alternate foot pattern.

Throwing: Progresses from two-handed throw to more sophisticated throw that includes body rotation and a forward shift of weight.

APPLICATION: KNOWLEDGE IN ACTION

1. Describe the way the 2 and 3-year-old children maneuver the stairs in the video. How will stair-climbing skills change over time?

2. Describe Olivia's hopping and jumping skills and her performance with the ball. Is her performance consistent with norms for her age? How will Olivia's hopping and jumping skills change over time? How will her throwing and catching skills change?

3. How does Olivia's attempt to catch a ball illustrate the proximodistal trend in motor development?

4. Outline developmental changes in the drawing and writing skills of children between the ages of 2 and 5. How do the children in the video illustrate these changes?

5. What activities are the children in the video participating in that facilitate fine motor development? What are the relative roles of maturation and learning in the development of fine motor skills, and how do these interact?

PIAGET'S PREOPERATIONAL STAGE

According to Jean Piaget, children enter the preoperational stage of cognitive development during the preschool years. The key feature of children's thinking in this stage is symbolic representation. The child is now able to use a symbol, an object, or a word to stand for something else. The use of symbols can be clearly seen in the child's use of language; for example, the child can now represent objects in the environment with the appropriate word and can refer to past and future events. The use of symbols is also apparent in children's drawings, imitation, mental imagery, and symbolic play. For example, a preoperational child might be observed feeding her doll imaginary cereal or drawing a picture of the balloons at her last birthday party.

Despite these increases in cognitive skills, the thought processes of preoperational children result in characteristic errors in reasoning. One of the most easily observed deficiencies is the tendency to view the world from one's own perspective only, a phenomenon that Piaget termed egocentrism. Because of egocentric thinking, preoperational children may "hide" by covering their eyes or only parts of their bodies, believing that if they can't see the seeker then they, themselves, can't be seen.

Other preoperational reasoning errors result from thinking that is intuitive, rather than logical. For example, preschool children are incapable of conservation – they do not understand that certain properties of objects, such as volume or mass, do not change just because the superficial appearance of the object changes. Preoperational children are not only tied to their perceptions, they are also unable to de-center their thinking, or think about more than one aspect of a problem at a time. Their thinking shows what Piaget called irreversibility—they are unable to reverse or mentally undo an action.

KEY TERMS AND CONCEPTS

Animism: The tendency to attribute life-like qualities to inanimate objects.

Centration: The tendency to concentrate on only one aspect of a situation or a problem at a time.

Egocentrism: The inability to take the perspective of another person, or to imagine the other person's point of view.

Failure to conserve: The inability to understand that objects stay the same in weight, volume, and other properties despite changes in shape or appearance.

Irreversibility: The inability to mentally reverse a series of events or operations back to the starting point.

Perception-bound thought: Being easily distracted by the concrete, observable characteristics of objects.

Preoperational stage: Piaget's stage of cognitive development marked by rapid growth in representational, or symbolic mental activity.

Transductive reasoning: Reasoning from particular event to particular event.

2 to 5
Early Childhood – Cognitive and
Language Development
Piaget's Preoperational Stage

Name _____

Section _____

APPLICATION: KNOWLEDGE IN ACTION

1. Describe Jean Piaget's preoperational stage of development. How does the ability to use mental symbols to represent objects change the way that children interact in the world? Describe the behaviors exhibited by the children in the video that illustrate representational or symbolic activity.

2. Using examples from the video, discuss Piaget's concept of egocentrism. Why are children in the preoperational stage more egocentric than older children, according to Piaget?

2 to 5
Early Childhood – Cognitive and
Language Development
Piaget's Preoperational Stage

Name _____

Section _____

3. What is conservation? Describe the conservation tasks shown in the video and discuss the performance of Olivia, Debra, Jacob, Christopher, and Jack. Are their responses typical of children in the preoperational stage? Why or why not?

4. How do Olivia, Debra, Jacob, Christopher, and Jack respond when asked to explain "why" they thought the amount of liquid or play dough had changed or not changed? How do these responses illustrate deficits in the reasoning abilities of preoperational children, as described by Piaget, including centration, irreversibility, perception-bound thought, and their focus on states rather than dynamic transformations?

LANGUAGE DEVELOPMENT

After the age of 2, children acquire new words at an astronomical rate. These rapid gains in children's vocabulary are accompanied by mastery of more complex grammatical structures such as forming past tenses and plurals. As children acquire the grammatical rules of their language, a type of error called overregularization may occur in which children overuse the basic rules of language. For example, a 2½ or 3-year-old child may say, "I bringed my Barbie," or "My feets are cold."

Children also become more likely to use correct syntax – that is, they become more aware of how words should be ordered to convey a particular meaning. By the age of 5, children are using more sophisticated grammar and producing adult-like sentences in which they are able to transform basic language structures into a variety of sentence forms, a process called transformational grammar. They have learned the rules to transform a basic idea such as, "I am going to the park" to the form of a question, "Am I going to the park?", a negative sentence, "I am not going to the park.", or an imperative, "Go to the park!"

KEY TERMS AND CONCEPTS

Grammatical morphemes: Word endings that impart grammatical information such as possession, plurals, and tense.

Overregularization: An error in which the basic rules of grammar are overused, such as adding the regular suffix "ed" to an irregular verb.

Pragmatics: Rules for the appropriate social use of language, allowing children to express ideas efficiently in a given context.

Referential communication skills: Learning to communicate clearly; that is, the ability to produce clear verbal messages and to ask for clarification when the meaning of other messages is unclear.

Semantic development: Acquisition of vocabulary, or the meanings behind words.

Transformational grammar: The ability to transform basic language structures into a variety of sentence forms.

APPLICATION: KNOWLEDGE IN ACTION

1. When does the vocabulary spurt begin? Why do researchers believe that children learn new words at such an astronomical rate?

2. How old does Debra say that she is? What error does she make in her articulation of her answer? Is this typical for a child her age? Why or why not?

2 to 5
Early Childhood – Cognitive and
Language Development
Language Development

Name _____

Section _____

3. What is a grammatical morpheme? Olivia and Christopher incorrectly add "ed" to refer to the past tense. What does this indicate regarding their mastery of the rules of English? How old do you think Christopher and Olivia are? Why?

4. Discuss the language achievements of early childhood in the context of Olivia's conversation with the interviewer.

PLAY

Between the ages of 2 and 5, children's social interactions become increasingly reciprocal and coordinated, which is reflected in their play. Children's play can be divided into four categories, ranging from least to most socially complex – nonsocial activity, parallel play, associative play, and cooperative play.

Nonsocial activity includes both solitary play and onlooker behavior in which a child plays alone or simply watches another child play without participating. Parallel play is not interactive – children play side-by-side, in close proximity to each other, but are focused on their own rather than the other's activities. In associative play children will share materials, and they may even organize their play around a common theme, such as cooking in the kitchen, but there is no coordinated purpose or goal. Cooperative play, by contrast, is goal-focused. It is organized group activity, both interactive and reciprocal. Children plan and assign roles, and work together to achieve a common purpose.

Around the age of 4 or 5 there is a developmental shift in the type of play in which children engage. Four and 5 year olds begin to demonstrate constructive play, drawing pictures or working on puzzles in pairs or groups, purposefully creating and constructing something together. Play also becomes more complex as children begin to experiment with both everyday and imaginary roles through pretend or dramatic play. This type of play involves advances in cognition, perspective taking, and communication skills.

KEY TERMS AND CONCEPTS

Associative play: Children share materials or organize their play around a common theme, but there is no coordinated purpose or goal.

Constructive play: Goal-focused play that involves purposefully creating or constructing something together.

Cooperative play: Goal-focused play that is both interactive and reciprocal; children plan and assign roles and work together to achieve a common purpose.

Dramatic play: A type of play in which children act out everyday and imaginary roles.

Nonsocial activity: Includes both solitary play and onlooker behavior in which a child plays alone or simply watches another child play without participating.

Parallel play: Children play side-by-side, in close proximity to each other, but are focused on their own rather than the other's activities.

APPLICATION: KNOWLEDGE IN ACTION

1. Describe the following play interactions depicted in the video: nonsocial activity, parallel play, associative play, and cooperative play, and discuss the differences between each play category.

2. Are nonsocial and parallel play seen only in young preschoolers? Why or why not? Often parents and teachers are concerned if a child spends a great deal of his or her time playing alone. Should we expect solitary play to decline with age? When is there cause for concern?

3. How is play behavior influenced by cognitive development? Describe the dramatic play exhibited by the children in the video. According to Piaget, what cognitive processes are required for imaginary play? Estimate the ages of the children engaging in dramatic and imaginary play. Which behaviors influence your estimates?

GENDER

Children's knowledge about gender and gender-role expectations develops very early. Preschoolers have a strong sense of gender identity, a sense of being male or female. And, between the ages of 4 and 6, children develop gender constancy, the realization that gender stays the same regardless of how one looks or behaves. At this point, they may adopt very rigid standards for what they believe is appropriate male and female dress and behavior.

Pre-school children are more likely to play with sex-appropriate toys; that is, boys are more likely to play with stereotypical "boy toys" – such as trucks and guns; and girls are more likely to play with stereotypical "girl toys" – such as dolls and kitchen sets. Over the preschool years, gender segregation also increases as children are more likely to play with same-sex peers rather than opposite-sex peers.

KEY TERMS AND CONCEPTS

Gender constancy: The realization that gender stays the same regardless of how one looks or behaves.

Gender identity: A sense of being male or female.

Gender role: Behaviors and psychological characteristics that are considered to be appropriate for each gender.

Gender schema theory: The theory that children develop ideas about what boys and girls do, which in turn influences perceptions and behaviors.

Gender segregation: A preference for same-sex playmates.

APPLICATION: KNOWLEDGE IN ACTION

1. When do children typically develop a sense of gender identity? When do they typically develop gender constancy? Do the children depicted in the video give responses that you would expect from a preschool child in regard to gender identity and constancy? Why or why not?

2. Do the children in the video show stereotypic gender role expectations? Cite examples to support your answer. How do children develop gender role stereotypes?

2 to 5
Early Childhood – Social and Emotional
Development
Gender

Name _____

Section _____

3. Are preschool children typically flexible or inflexible in their ideas regarding gender typed behavior? Why? Give examples from the video that are consistent with your response.

CONNECTING CONTENT: RESEARCH AND THEORIES AND ACTION

Summary of Observation Module Content

- Preschool children in gym.
- Three girls in preschool classroom doing a puzzle.
- Olivia, age 3 and Sarah, age 5, talking to interviewer.
- Brianna and Jacob in preschool classroom.
- Olivia, age 3, and mom playing a board game.
- Three boys in preschool classroom building with blocks.
- Interview 1: Debra, age 3.
- Interview 2: Jack, age 5.

Observation Module Questions 2 to 5 Years	Name _____ Section _____

1. Compare Olivia's and Sarah's facility with language as they relay past events. How do language and cognition interact in development? Discuss this interaction from the perspectives of Piaget and Vygotsky.

Observation Module Questions	Name _____
2 – 5 Years	Section _____

2. In the video, Brianna is crying and says that Jacob hurt her feelings. Why is Brianna upset? Based on Brianna's response to the teacher's attempt to intervene, how old would you say Brianna is? In what stage of cognitive development would you place her, according to Piaget? Why?

3. Describe the different types of play depicted in the video. What is the relationship between play and a child's social competency with peers in early childhood? Using specific examples from the video, discuss how play contributes to advances in communication skills, perspective taking, and emotional understanding in early childhood.

4. In the video, Olivia's mother helps her play a game. How would Vygotsky describe this interaction? Discuss the zone of proximal development and scaffolding, using Olivia and her mother as examples.

5. Describe video illustrations of the following: episodic or event memory, cued vs. free recall, suggestibility, and false memories. From an information processing perspective, are these children typical? Will their memory strategies likely change with age? In what ways? Can more efficient memory strategies be taught to young children? What does this indicate about the development of memory?

6. Describe the responses of Debra and Jack when they are presented with two of Piaget's classic conservation tasks. Why was it necessary for Debra to agree that the two balls of play dough were exactly equal in amount? What characteristic preoperational reasoning errors can you identify? Can conservation be taught? How would Vygotsky approach the task of teaching a young child to conserve?

7. Indicate Jack's responses to the following: "Tell me three things about yourself. Who is your best friend and why?" If this were all the information you had about Jack, would you still be able to estimate his age and level of cognitive development according to Piaget? Why or why not?

8. One criticism of Piaget is that his conservation tasks do not account for the social dynamics of the testing situation or the linguistic difficulties a child in the preoperatonal period may experience. For example, a child may or may not understand the questions posed by the examiner and even small changes in the way a questions is asked may lead them to believe that a particular answer is expected of them. Listen carefully to the examiner as he presents the conservation tasks to Debra and Jack. Are there aspects of this testing situation that may have misled the children being tested and/or caused them to respond in a particular way?

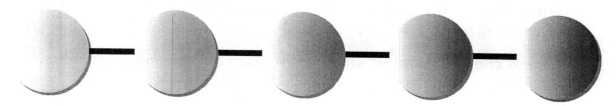

OBSERVING CHILDREN AND ADOLESCENTS 5 TO 11 YEARS

GROSS AND FINE MOTOR DEVELOPMENT

During middle childhood, children continue to improve in coordination of both fine and gross motor activities. In general, gross motor skills such as throwing, catching, running, jumping, and kicking are executed more efficiently, with more strength, speed, coordination, and balance than in younger years. In addition, eye-hand coordination increases and reaction times decrease, impacting the child's ability to coordinate motor and visual information. These improvements in coordination and timing enhance the child's performance in all kinds of sports, but there is much individual variation in motor development, which can affect athletic prowess.

Fine motor development also continues in the middle childhood period, particularly impacting writing ability. Kindergarteners move their wrists and arms while using markers, not yet having developed the fine motor control that will allow them to use more refined finger movements. By second grade, pencil control improves, as children gain better control of their small motor movements and, eventually, they are able to manipulate a pencil using only their fingers. These changes allow handwriting to become more fluid and legible, and children are better able to play sports and games requiring these more refined skills. Boys will usually outperform girls in gross motor skills, whereas girls typically perform better than boys in fine motor skills.

KEY TERMS AND CONCEPTS

Agility: Quickness and accuracy of movements.

Balance: Maintaining equilibrium of the body when it is in various positions.

Coordination: Integrating motor movements with sensory information or other motor movements.

Eye-hand coordination: Ability to coordinate fine movements using visual information.

Flexibility: Bending of the body across a normal range of motions.

Reaction time: Time it takes to initiate movement in response to a stimulus.

APPLICATION: KNOWLEDGE IN ACTION

1. How does gross motor development impact eye-hand coordination and reaction times? Discuss your answer in the context of the throwing and catching skills of John, Sam, and Rachel.

2. Outline the major changes in gross motor development in middle childhood. Using examples from the video, discuss individual differences in motor performance.

3. Discuss the developmental progression of fine motor skills in middle childhood. How do these changes impact drawing and writing? Cite examples from the video to support your answer.

4. Are there sex differences in motor development in middle childhood? How might these differences affect social functioning?

5 to 11
Middle Childhood – Physical
Development
Gross and Fine Motor

Name _____

Section _____

5. Why is visual motor integration important in middle childhood? Give examples from the video of activities that depend on the coordination of visual perception and motor skills. Do children develop the ability to coordinate visual and motor activity through maturation or learning? What are some activities that a child can engage in which will facilitate the development of visual motor integration?

PIAGET'S CONCRETE OPERATIONAL STAGE

In middle childhood, children show dramatic changes in their thinking, entering what Piaget called the concrete operational stage of cognitive development. During the concrete operational stage, children begin to use logical instead of intuitive, perception-bound reasoning. They are no longer fooled, for example, by Piaget's classic conservation tasks.

When children in the concrete operational stage are asked why they believe that the taller glass or the flattened play dough contains the same amount, their explanations illustrate that they are now able to de-center, or to think about more than one aspect of a problem at a time. They are able to follow the transformation from beginning to end and to mentally reverse the process, achieving a logical milestone that Piaget called reversibility.

While these new cognitive abilities allow children to more effectively operate in their worlds, they continue to have difficulty with problems and ideas that they have not experienced directly, a skill which will not emerge until they reach Piaget's final stage of cognitive development, formal operations.

KEY TERMS AND CONCEPTS

Concrete operational stage: The stage of cognitive development in which children begin to use logical instead of intuitive, perception-bound reasoning.

Conservation: The ability to understand that objects stay the same in weight, volume, and other properties despite changes in shape or appearance.

Decentration: The ability to think about more than one aspect of a problem at a time.

Hierarchical classification: Understanding that some categories are superodinate and others subordinate.

Horizontal decalage: The ability to solve conservation problems in some contexts, but not in others.

Mental seriation: According to Piaget, the ability to order items along a quantitative dimension.

Reversibility: The ability to mentally reverse transformations of an object, according to Piaget.

APPLICATION: KNOWLEDGE IN ACTION

1. What is conservation? Why is the ability to conserve an important milestone in cognitive development, according to Piaget? Describe the conservation tasks and discuss the performance of the children depicted in the video. Are their responses typical of children in the concrete operational stage? Why or why not?

2. Cite specific reasons given by children in the video when they are asked to explain "why" they thought the amount of liquid or play dough had changed or not changed. How do these responses illustrate changes in the reasoning abilities of concrete operational children as described by Piaget? Include the following Piagetian concepts in your discussion: conservation, decentration, and reversibility.

3. Do the children in the video use logical or intuitive approaches to solving problems? Is their reasoning perception bound? Cite specific examples from the video that support your conclusion.

4. Are children in Piaget's concrete operational stage likely to be able to use their reasoning skills on problems and ideas that they have not experienced directly? Why or why not?

LEV VYGOTSKY: THE ZONE OF PROXIMAL DEVELOPMENT AND SCAFFOLDING

According to Lev Vygotsky, children's learning takes place within the zone of proximal development – the difference between what a child can do alone, without guidance, and what a child can do with help. A child's level of independent problem solving may be quite different than what he or she can learn or accomplish with the guidance and assistance of others – parents, teachers, and peers.

Gradually, through appropriate instruction, what a child can do one day with assistance becomes what a child can do independently. One instructional method designed to draw on the zone of proximal development is scaffolding. Scaffolding is a method in which assistance by more knowledgeable others is aimed slightly above what the child can do on his or her own – creating an environment that actually enhances children's learning. As the child becomes more competent, the supports are gradually removed and the child takes over. Scaffolding can take many forms including clear instructions, hints, prompts, reminders, demonstrations, and encouragement.

KEY TERMS AND CONCEPTS

Cooperative learning: A teaching method that involves grouping children together of different ability levels and having them work together, helping each other to achieve a common goal.

Scaffolding: The process of guiding a child, leading to a higher level of performance than the child could attain alone; scaffolding involves support and guidance in the form of explanations, demonstrations, and other prompts.

Sociocultural theory: Vygotstky's theory that stresses the important role of society and culture in development.

Zone of proximal development: The distance, or area, between a child's level of independent performance and performance with adult guidance or collaboration with a more capable peer.

5 to 11
Middle Childhood – Cognitive Development
Lev Vygotsky: The Zone of Proximal Development and Scaffolding

Name _____

Section _____

APPLICATION: KNOWLEDGE IN ACTION

1. In the video, we see two students of different ability levels reading together. Discuss the role of social interaction in children's learning. Why is cooperative learning an effective instructional tool?

2. How does scaffolding relate to Vygotsky's notion of the zone of proximal development? Does scaffolding always involve social interaction? Is scaffolding always performed by an adult? Discuss how the 5th grade teacher in the video uses scaffolding to guide her students in a learning activity.

5 to 11
Middle Childhood – Cognitive Development
Lev Vygotsky: The Zone of Proximal Development and Scaffolding

Name _____
Section _____

3. In what ways can assistance from a knowledgeable other impede a child's progress? How does this relate to the zone of proximal development?

MEMORY

REHEARSAL STRATEGIES AND SUGGESTIBILITY

As children age, they develop more memory strategies and become more adept at applying them. Rehearsal is a simple and effective memory strategy involving the repeating of information to be remembered. Research indicates that preschool children rarely rehearse information, but by middle childhood, rehearsal is a commonly used memory strategy. Older children are also more likely than younger children to rehearse clusters of information, as opposed to individual pieces of information, a strategy known as chunking. Chunking information increases the amount of information that can be rehearsed, thereby increasing efficiency.

The cognitive advances of middle childhood lead to other memory-enhancing strategies. For example, at about age 9 or 10, children begin to rely on categorization to remember long lists or to group items together; that is, they group information to be remembered semantically, into distinct, meaningful categories that make the information easier to remember. Older children are also more likely to use elaboration, adding new information to memory by associating it with information that is already stored. Elaboration is rarely used by younger children, probably because of their more limited knowledge base.

When shown a picture of two people, neither of whom are wearing hats, children between the ages of 5 and 11 are susceptible to creating false memories when asked leading questions, but somewhat less so than younger children. While memory suggestibility generally decreases with age, there is much individual variability with regard to the creation of false memories, as can be seen in the responses of Brian, Nathaniel, Sahara, and Beckett.

KEY TERMS AND CONCEPTS

Cued recall: Remembering information when given retrieval cues.

Elaboration: Adding new information to memory by associating it with information that is already stored.

Event memory: Memories based in the context of episodes or events.

Free recall: Remembering information without retrieval cues.

Metamemory: Knowledge of one's own memory processes.

Mnemonics: Technique used as a memory aid, such as a rhyme or formula.

Organization: Memory strategy involving arranging information based on relationships between items.

Rehearsal: A memory strategy that involves repeating information to be remembered.

Suggestibility: Recalling incorrect facts when prompted with specific cues.

APPLICATION: KNOWLEDGE IN ACTION

1. What strategies do children use in middle childhood to retain information in memory? What strategies do Drew and Jenny use to remember a list of words? Who uses a more efficient strategy, Drew or Jenny? Why? How do you expect their memory strategies will change with age?

2. Can more efficient memory strategies be taught to young children? Why or why not?

3. In the video, children are asked to look at a picture in a book and describe it to the interviewer. Although neither of the two people in the picture is wearing a hat, many of the children inaccurately recall the color of the hat when asked about it by the interviewer. How does the form of the question the interviewer asks influence their responses?

4. Why is research on memory suggestibility important? In what ways can we ask questions to decrease the likelihood of the creation of false memories in young children?

SELF-CONCEPT

As children progress through middle childhood, they show changes in their self-concepts - their thoughts about, and ways of describing, themselves. In early childhood, self-concept is very concrete and physical, and children focus on observable, overt characteristics. As they progress through middle childhood, children are more likely to describe themselves in terms of psychological and social qualities and to make social comparisons, greatly influencing self-esteem.

Self-esteem or a child's sense of self-worth develops in the context of social experiences. In early childhood, children evaluate themselves along two broad aspects of self-esteem: competence, both physical and cognitive, and personal and social adequacy. By mid-elementary school, five aspects of self-esteem emerge in children's self-evaluations: scholastic competence, athletic competence, physical appearance, behavioral conduct, and social acceptance. Self-esteem has been shown to be influenced by parents, teachers, and peers, and high self-esteem is positively related to social and academic success.

KEY TERMS AND CONCEPTS

Industry vs. Inferiority: Erikson's competency-based psychosocial crisis experienced by school age children.

Psychological traits: Conceptions of self that are not physical or possession-based, such as personal attributes, attitudes and beliefs.

Self-concept: Thoughts about and ways of describing oneself.

Self-esteem: Evaluations or judgments regarding the competencies of oneself.

Social comparisons: Evaluating oneself based on the perceptions of others.

5 to 11
**Middle Childhood – Social, Emotional
and Moral Development**
Self-concept

Name _____

Section _____

APPLICATION: KNOWLEDGE IN ACTION

1. When asked to describe themselves by telling three things about themselves, the responses of Todd and Christopher are very different from the responses of Rachel, Stephanie, and Ricardo. How do each of these children describe themselves? Based on these self-descriptions, how old would you estimate the children to be? Why?

2. What evidence of social comparison is present in the responses of the children in the video? How are social comparisons related to a child's self-esteem?

3. When do children begin to incorporate psychological traits into their self-descriptions? How does this relate to cognitive development?

4. Do the children in the video show age-related differences in their descriptions of themselves? In what ways does self-concept typically change over the course of middle childhood?

PEER ACCEPTANCE

As children move through middle childhood, relationships with peers become increasingly important. Some children are easily accepted by others, while others are more likely to experience rejection. Research shows that a number of qualities are related to popularity, including physical attractiveness, friendliness, and size or strength; while children who are described as "aggressive" or "different" are more likely to experience rejection.

Early friendships are typically based on playing together – the "best friends" of preschoolers are often those with whom they are in contact the most. School-age children between the ages of 6 and 8 describe friends as those who share, act nice, and are fun to be with. By age 8 to 10 children begin to consider personal qualities, and friends are described as those who are helpful, reliable, and trustworthy.

At all ages, status within a peer group is an important determinant of later adjustment. A child's popularity reflects his or her status within the group. A child's status or popularity within a group is largely determined by social behavior – children who are aggressive and disruptive, or alternatively, withdrawn and socially awkward are often rejected rather than accepted by their peers.

KEY TERMS AND CONCEPTS

Controversial children: Liked by some children and disliked by others.

Friendship: A social bond between two children.

Neglected children: Not popular or disliked, but rather overlooked by peers.

Peer group: Social group with behavioral norms where a child regularly associates with other children and feels group membership.

Popular children: Well-liked by most other children in the peer group.

Rejected children: Disliked by most other children in the peer group.

APPLICATION: KNOWLEDGE IN ACTION

1. How do the children in the video describe the "most liked child in class"? What factors appear to be influential in determining popularity in middle childhood? What determines rejection or acceptance?

2. In what way does peer status influence conceptions of self? Do the responses of the children in the video regarding their self-concepts give clues regarding their perceptions of their own peer status?

3. How are peer acceptance and popularity related to other competencies?

4. Are social behaviors valued differently cross-culturally? Might behaviors that predict acceptance in the United States predict rejection in other cultures? Why or why not?

GENDER

By middle childhood, children have acquired many gender stereotypes, and describe boys and girls differently. Six to11 year olds are also likely to express different gender role expectations for males and females.

During the middle childhood years, many children become aware that there are exceptions to gender stereotypes and their beliefs about what it means to be male or female become more flexible. Although there is increased recognition of the flexibility of sex-roles, gender-typed behavior is still the rule rather than the exception, particularly for boys. The behavior of boys becomes even more gender-typed, and they engage increasingly in masculine-type activities. Girls, on the other hand, are more androgynous at this age and are likely to participate in cross-gender activities such as baseball and show an interest in cross-gender toys and games.

KEY TERMS AND CONCEPTS

Gender constancy: Knowledge that one will always be a male or a female.

Gender identity: Knowledge of being a male or a female.

Gender role expectations: Expected behavior patterns and psychological characteristics for each gender.

Gender-typed behavior: Engaging in activities typically associated with one's own sex.

Gender stereotypes: Widely held beliefs that males and females will choose to engage in gender-typed activities.

APPLICATION: KNOWLEDGE IN ACTION

1. Describe the responses of the children in the video to the questions, "What are girls like?" and "What are boys like?" Do their responses indicate that they have acquired gender role stereotypes? Why or why not?

2. Do the children in the video express different gender role expectations for males and females in their responses to the "Barbie and Ken" questions? Discuss the roles of family, education, and culture in their perceptions.

3. Which children in the video are more flexible in their ideas regarding gender role stereotypes? Describe the responses of children depicted in the video that are consistent with your response. Why are some children more flexible than others with regard to gender role stereotypes? Would you expect boys or girls to be more flexible in this regard? Why?

4. Discuss sex differences in gender typed behavior. Why are these differences more pronounced for boys than girls in middle childhood?

MORAL DEVELOPMENT

The basis of children's reasoning and judgments about moral decisions changes over time, a concept explored by Lawrence Kohlberg in his theory of moral development. Moral decisions in middle childhood generally reflect either a punishment-reward orientation or the desire to obey rules and conform to social norms, reasoning styles that Kohlberg labeled preconventional and conventional.

In early and middle childhood, children's standards for moral behavior are governed primarily by external consequences; that is, punishment or reinforcement. As a result, moral behavior may be inconsistent and vary from one situation to the next, with factors such as the likelihood of being caught and peer pressure having an impact on moral decision-making.

In the early years of middle childhood, children tend to judge acts as unilaterally right or wrong and to focus on rules and consequences, with intentions often neglected, a reasoning style that Piaget labeled heteronomous morality. As children approach the end of middle childhood, they are only beginning to reach autonomous morality, questioning the absolute nature of laws and rules and considering the impact of intentions on moral decisions.

KEY TERMS AND CONCEPTS

Autonomous morality: Judgments of morality based on intent or human need, rather than objective consequences.

Conventional level: Moral decisions are based on gaining approval and praise from others and conforming to social norms.

Good boy-nice girl orientation: Stage 3, conventional level, in which an individual behaves morally to gain approval and acceptance from other people.

Heteronomous morality: Early moral development where rules are seen as absolutes.

Law and order orientation: Stage 4, conventional level, in which an individual emphasizes the importance of abiding by laws and maintaining social order.

Personal reward orientation: Stage 2, preconventional level, in which an individual obeys rules to receive rewards.

Preconventional level: Morality is based on external factors; the focus is on rules and the consequences for breaking them.

Punishment-obedience orientation: Stage 1, preconventional level, in which an individual obeys rules to avoid punishment.

5 to 11
**Middle Childhood – Social, Emotional
and Moral Development**
Moral Development

Name _____

Section _____

APPLICATION: KNOWLEDGE IN ACTION

1. When asked to respond to Kohlberg's Heinz dilemma, do all of the children in the video judge that it is wrong for Heinz to steal the drug? Are their responses typical for middle childhood? Can you determine whether these children are reasoning at a preconventional, conventional, or postconventional level from their yes or no responses? Why or why not?

2. Describe the responses of the children in the video when asked *why* it was right or wrong for Heinz to steal the drug. Are their responses consistent with preconventional, conventional, or postconventional reasoning? On what basis did you make this decision?

3. Which of the responses of the children in the video indicates that they are beginning to question the absolute nature of laws and rules and to consider the impact of intentions on moral decisions? How does this relate to Piaget's concepts of moral realism and moral relativism?

DEVELOPMENTAL DISABILITIES

While there are individual differences in development, most children develop typically. Some children, however, may show significant maturational delays or differences – these children are often diagnosed with developmental disabilities. Developmental differences are frequently referred to as exceptionalities, an inclusive term for a wide variety of conditions, including Mental Retardation and Pervasive Developmental Disorders.

Derek, for example, has Down's Syndrome. He has many delays in his development, yet he is able to participate in and enjoy activities in his classroom, and the other students in class clearly feel that he is a member of their group. Michaela has a different exceptionality, Asperger's disorder, a Pervasive Developmental Disorder that involves difficulty in relating to other people, as can be seen when she interacts with her classmates. Although she has trouble interacting with her classmates, they seek to include her in activities and to assist her whenever possible.

Many developmental disabilities are diagnosed based on delays or differences from what we know of typical development, and different labels are used to describe the patterns of difference. It is important to remember, however, that a child with a disability is first and foremost a child, and that all children are typical in many ways.

KEY TERMS AND CONCEPTS

Asperger's disorder: Autism spectrum disorder characterized by impairments in socialization and stereotypic behavior, without language deficits.

Developmental disabilities: Term used to describe children who have a limitation due to a loss or reduction of function.

Down's Syndrome: Most common genetically based developmental disability caused in most cases by a third chromosome.

Exceptionality: Describes developmental difference without negative connotations.

Inclusion: Having students with disabilities educated in the community of those without disabilities.

Pervasive Developmental Disorder: Autism spectrum disorders, characterized by stereotypic behaviors and deficits in socialization and language.

APPLICATION: KNOWLEDGE IN ACTION

1. Describe Derek's physical features. Are these characteristics typical of children with Down's Syndrome?

2. Derek has Trisomy 21, the most common form of Down's Syndrome. Are there other forms of Down's Syndrome? Do they present differently? Why or why not?

3. Describe Derek's interaction with his peers in the classroom. Does it appear that he is accepted by others in his class? Do you think his inclusion placement is likely a positive experience? Why or why not?

4. Describe Michaela's behavior as she interacts with her peers. Does she seek out social interaction with others? Are other children able to engage her in interactive activities? How does she respond when they try to do so?

5. The Pervasive Developmental Disorders are characterized by deficits in social relatedness, language abnormalities, and stereotypic behaviors. Describe Michaela's behavior in each of these areas. How is her behavior atypical for a child her age?

CONNECTING CONTENT: RESEARCH AND THEORIES IN ACTION

Summary of Observation Module Content

- Interview 1: Drew, age 10.
- Interview 2: Rachel, age 9.
- Developmental Disabilities: Derek, age 7, and Michaela, age 7.

Observation Module Questions
5 to 11 Years

Name _____

Section _____

1. Children go through many changes during the period of growth known as middle childhood. Have Drew and Rachel reached the norms and milestones that characterize "typical" development in middle childhood? Why or why not? Cite specific responses to interview questions that support your conclusion in regard to their level of cognitive, social, emotional, and moral development.

2. Are the number and counting skills exhibited by Derek typical for a 7-year-old child? Why or why not? Has he developed one-to-one correspondence? Has he acquired the principle of cardinality? Based on Derek's skill level, at what age is he functioning developmentally?

3. Children like Michaela, who are diagnosed with Asperger's, often have language abilities that are typical for their age, but seldom use language interactively in social situations. Discuss how Michaela's use of language differs from other children her age.

OBSERVING CHILDREN AND ADOLESCENTS 12 TO 18 YEARS

SECTION 1: ADOLESCENCE: PHYSICAL DEVELOPMENT

PUBERTY AND BODY IMAGE

With the onset of puberty, dramatic physical changes occur. There is much individual variability in the age of onset of puberty, and differences in height and weight changes, as well as in the development of secondary sex characteristics, can lead to striking contrasts in the appearance of adolescents who are the same age.

Sex differences at the onset of puberty are readily apparent, with females generally entering puberty earlier than males. Research shows that age of onset of puberty may significantly impact social and emotional functioning, with differential effects for males and females. Changes in body mass composition that occur along with hormonal changes are also different for males and females and may impact body image.

KEY TERMS AND CONCEPTS

Body image: Evaluative ideas about one's physical appearance.

Early maturation: Physical and sexual maturity reached prior to peers.

Growth spurt: Dramatic increases in height and weight as children enter adolescence.

Late maturation: Physical and sexual maturity reached later than peers.

Menarche: Time of first menstruation.

Primary sexual characteristics: Physical difference between males and females that are present prior to puberty.

Puberty: Sexual maturity characterized by reproductive capability.

Secondary sex characteristics: Physical differences between males and females related to sexual maturation.

Spermarche: Time of first ejaculation.

APPLICATION: KNOWLEDGE IN ACTION

1. Do males and females reach puberty at the same age? Describe the physical differences among the adolescents presented in the video. How do these differences likely influence their social functioning?

2. How does the timing of puberty influence adolescent adjustment? Discuss the differential effects of early and late maturation for males and females.

12 to 18
**Adolescence – Physical
Development**
Puberty and Body Image

Name _____

Section _____

3. How do the physical changes of adolescence impact body image? Why are females more likely than males to have a negative body image? Are the responses of the adolescent girls in the video consistent with the research on body image and self-concept? Why or why not?

PIAGET'S FORMAL OPERATIONAL STAGE

ABSTRACTION, HYPOTHETICAL PROPOSITIONS, AND RISK-TAKING

The formal operational stage of cognitive development is reached when an adolescent begins to think abstractly and to reason hypothetically. In this stage of cognitive development, logical abilities can be applied to both real and imagined scenarios. Adolescents also begin to use what Piaget called hypothetico-deductive reasoning; that is, they approach hypothetical problems in much the same way as a person using the scientific method, systematically generating and evaluating potential solutions.

While these new cognitive abilities open up a world of possibilities for the formal operational thinker, they may also play a role in some of the less pleasant aspects of the adolescent experience. As adolescents begin to think in terms of possibilities, they may have more difficulty accepting the world as it is, criticizing rules or authority and envisioning an alternate or more perfect reality. This idealism may result in considerable frustration for an adolescent, as the world does not always cooperate with their logical alternatives.

Some of this frustration is due to a heightening of egocentrism in early adolescence. Many young adolescents, armed with their newly developed hypothetical reasoning skills, have difficulty recognizing that others may not share the same set of assumptions or ideas regarding alternative possibilities. As they mature, they begin to discover that they must consider and adapt to the ideas of others. As adolescents begin to have consideration for the thoughts of others, yet continue to be somewhat egocentric in their thinking, a phenomenon known as the imaginary audience emerges – an adolescent's belief that the thoughts of others mirror one's own. For example, a teenage girl walking alone across the cafeteria may think that everyone is looking at her hair, when really, she is the only one thinking about her hairstyle.

A second manifestation of adolescent egocentrism is a phenomenon known as the personal fable. This is the belief that one's experiences are unique and original, that no one else has ever, for example, been quite as in love in the history of the world. Adolescents may also believe that they are invulnerable to harm due to the personal fable – the fact that cigarette smoking causes cancer, for example, doesn't really apply to them. This may explain the increases in risk-taking behavior often seen in adolescence.

KEY TERMS AND CONCEPTS

Formal operational stage: Cognitive stage in which thinking is no longer tied to the observable or factual.

Hypothetico-deductive reasoning: Logical reasoning about hypothetical situations or ideas that is characterized by starting with a general hypothesis and deducing a specific hypothesis.

Imaginary audience: Adolescent tendency to feel as if "on stage" before a critical audience that is focused on them uniquely.

Personal fable: The belief that individual experiences are unique and original, which can contribute to increased risk-taking behavior.

12 to 18
Adolescence – Cognitive
Development
Piaget's Formal Operational Stage

Name _____

Section _____

APPLICATION: KNOWLEDGE IN ACTION

1. Compare the responses of Julor, Jenny, and Alan to the hypothetical question, "What if people had no thumbs?" Which of these children has reached Piaget's formal operational stage of cognitive development? On what basis did you make this decision?

2. What is hypothetico-deductive reasoning? Do any of the children in the video use hypothetico-deductive reasoning to arrive at conclusions regarding the "no thumbs" question? Cite specific characteristics of their response that support your answer.

3. Describe the responses of Alan, Maria, and other adolescents in the video to questions regarding drinking and driving and unprotected sex. How do they explain these risk-taking behaviors? Discuss their responses in terms of Piaget's personal fable concept.

SELF-CONCEPT

IDENTITY FORMATION

Adolescents are trying to figure out who they are and where they belong. They are becoming unique individuals, separate from the family, who often experiment with different looks, styles, and attitudes.

A major challenge in the development of self occurs during adolescence – the task of forming an identity. The attainment of a strong sense of identity is a process rather than a simple step on the path toward adulthood. According to Erikson, adolescents are challenged to find a balance between trying out many identity possibilities and choosing a consistent self. The central challenge for an adolescent is answering the question, "Who am I?", in Erikson's identity versus identity diffusion stage. Fantasy is frequently employed as a tool to aid identity development, in which an adolescent envisions possible alternatives in a variety of different dimensions such as occupational choice, relationship status, and religious or political affiliations. Adolescents may achieve a consistent identity in some or all of the different aspects of self, often resolving the identity crisis in some areas before others.

Recent research suggests that adolescents progress through different stages in the formation of identity. James Marcia has outlined four identity statuses, each reflecting a different balance between being able to establish a consistent self and having difficulty in establishing an identity. Achievement occurs when a person has explored different identity possibilities and has purposefully chosen a particular identity.

KEY TERMS AND CONCEPTS

Identity achievement: One of Marcia's identity statuses involving resolution of the identity crisis by making commitments to particular goals and beliefs.

Identity diffusion: One of Marcia's identity statuses in which there is no commitment to an identity or attempt to arrive at a commitment.

Identity foreclosure: One of Marcia's identity statuses involving commitment to an identity without active exploration of alternatives.

Identity versus identity diffusion: One psychosocial stage during adolescence, according to Erikson, in which adolescents are challenged to find a balance between trying out many identity possibilities and choosing a consistent self.

Moratorium: One of Marcia's identity statuses involving active exploration of identity alternatives.

12 to 18
Adolescence – Social, Emotional,
And Moral Development
Self-concept – Identity Formation

Name _____

Section _____

APPLICATION: KNOWLEDGE IN ACTION

1. Describe the different looks and styles and the adolescents' use of slang on the video. Are these adolescents having an identity crisis? Using specific examples from the video, discuss your answer in the context of the psychological conflict that Erikson called identity versus identity diffusion.

2. When the adolescents in the video are asked what they have planned for their lives, their responses illustrate significant individual differences in identity development. Describe each of their responses in terms of Marcia's identity statuses.

12 to 18
Adolescence – Social, Emotional,
And Moral Development
Self-concept – Identity Formation

Name _____

Section _____

3. Given the identity statuses of each of the individuals in the video, what would you predict regarding their social and emotional adjustment? Why?

4. Are the adolescents in the video likely to change their ideas regarding identity in the future? Is identity formation a distinct phase of development or a gradual process?

PEERS AND DOMAIN INFLUENCES

The influence of peers increases dramatically during adolescence, although research shows that this influence is often domain specific, with parents continuing to have more influence in some areas of an adolescent's life and peers having more influence in others.

Research indicates that in early adolescence, children begin to decrease dependence on parents for social support, expanding the range of social relationships and influence. This trend continues throughout adolescence, although family members continue to provide a central base of support in healthy teen-parent relationships. During adolescence, young people and their parents must adapt to the increasing need for self-reliance on the part of the adolescent. Periodic conflict may emerge as the adolescent becomes more assertive about his or her own ideas or choices; however, the impact of this conflict is largely dependent on the quality of the parent-child relationship.

Parenting practices have also been shown to affect adolescent behavior, as has crowd affiliation. In general, achievement oriented parents are likely to have children with higher grades, while parents who show low levels of parental monitoring and an absence of joint decision making are likely to have children who are low in self-reliance and more prone to drug use. Peer group membership is strongly influenced by both academic achievement and drug use, thus parental involvement in an adolescent's life has an impact on his or her peer relationships.

KEY TERMS AND CONCEPTS

Achievement-oriented parents: Parents who exhibit high expectations regarding the academic achievement of their children.

Domain influences: Influence in a specific area of a child's behavior, such as academic achievement or drug and alcohol use.

Joint decision-making: Style of parent-child interaction whereby both children and parents have a voice in decisions regarding the child's life.

Parental monitoring: Seeking awareness of and supervising a child's behavior.

Quality of parent-child relationship: The closeness of the relationship between a parent and a child, which impacts the relative influence of peers and parents.

12 to 18
Adolescence – Social, Emotional,
And Moral Development
Peers and Domain Influences

Name _____

Section _____

APPLICATION: KNOWLEDGE IN ACTION

1. How do peer relationships change in adolescence? How do adolescents benefit socially and emotionally from close friendships?

2. Describe the responses of the high school seniors presented in the video to the question, "Who has more influence in your life?" Which areas of their lives are more influenced by parents? Are their responses consistent with research findings on the relative influence of parents and peers in adolescence? Why or why not?

12 to 18
Adolescence – Social, Emotional,
And Moral Development
Peers and Domain Influences

Name _____

Section _____

3. How does parenting style influence the relative influence of parents and peers in adolescence?

CLIQUES, CROWDS, AND CONFORMITY

Over the course of adolescence, changes in peer group structures take place, with same-sex cliques who are in close association with one another developing into crowds – clearly observable peer cultures whose members exhibit behavioral, personality, and appearance-based similarities. All high schools have cliques and crowds, although the labels that they use may differ.

Cliques are small groups of friends who interact with one another frequently, providing social support for one another. In late childhood, cliques are usually same-sex groups, while heterosexual cliques develop in early adolescence. These mixed-sex groups of friends pave the way toward another peer group structure: the crowd.

A crowd is a collection of heterosexual cliques that share characteristics or participate in similar activities. High schools may have different names for crowds, but they exist in every high school. Labels such as "brains," "populars," "druggies," "losers," "jocks," and "normals" are common examples. While the rules for membership are not explicitly articulated, crowds appear to include or exclude others based on consistent standards. Research shows that crowd membership is influenced by many variables, including physical attractiveness, grades, use of drugs and alcohol, involvement in aggressive activity, and involvement in sports and social activities.

Thus, cliques and crowds are social structures that have norms or expectations that must be met by members. Individuals may move in and out of different social groups during adolescence for a variety of reasons, but it appears that changing one's clique is more easily achieved than changing one's crowd identity.

Since cliques and crowds have unspoken, yet consistent, rules for membership, conformity, or yielding to the opinions or wishes of others, is an important variable in adolescent social structures. Conformity to peers increases steadily in early adolescence, while conformity to parental wishes declines. As adolescents begin to establish self-reliance, the influence of both parents and peers diminishes.

KEY TERMS AND CONCEPTS

Cliques: Small groups of friends who interact with one another frequently, providing social support for one another.

Conformity: Yielding to the opinions or wishes of others.

Crowds: A collection of heterosexual cliques that share characteristics or participate in similar activities.

Peer group structures: Social groups that have norms or expectations that must be met by members.

Peer pressure: Peer expectations for one's behavior that may influence choices.

12 to 18

Adolescence – Social, Emotional,
And Moral Development
Cliques, Crowds, and Conformity

Name _____

Section _____

APPLICATION: KNOWLEDGE IN ACTION

1. What is the difference between a clique and a crowd? Are the social structures described by the adolescents in the video cliques or crowds? Cite specific examples from the video to support your answer.

2. Are rules for membership in adolescent social structures clearly articulated or implicit? Are the adolescents in the video able to easily outline the norms that must be met by members of a specific social group? Why or why not?

12 to 18
Adolescence – Social, Emotional,
And Moral Development
Peers and Domain Influences

Name _____

Section _____

3. Does conformity to peers increase or decrease over the course of adolescence? What factors contribute to peer conformity in adolescence?

MORAL DEVELOPMENT

When adolescents begin to think more abstractly and become better able to take another's perspective, they also become better able to consider multiple perspectives and to use their own ethical principles when presented with a moral dilemma. Research indicates that there are developmental trends in moral reasoning, as Lawrence Kohlberg proposed. Studies show that preconventional, reward-punishment based reasoning decreases significantly during the adolescent years, with most adolescents reasoning at the conventional level by age 16.

At the conventional level, moral decisions are based on gaining approval and praise from others and conforming to social norms. During early adolescence, most individuals begin to make moral judgments based on concern for being "good", while older adolescents begin to incorporate moral standards that parents or authority figures have taught them. Morality may also become an important component of an adolescent's identity, with research indicating that many adolescents desire to see themselves as honest, fair, and caring.

Postconventional reasoning involves moral decision making that is based on a set of broad ethical principles, which may transcend social rules and laws. Early postconventional reasoning is characterized by viewing laws as social contracts that may be compromised if a person's individual rights are violated, while the final stage of postconventional reasoning involves self-chosen ethical principles of universal justice for all humans that transcend conflicting laws or social contracts. It should be noted that research indicates that Kohlberg's postconventional level of moral reasoning is often not attained until adulthood, and very few adults reach the final stage of postconventional reasoning.

KEY TERMS AND CONCEPTS

Conventional level: Moral decisions are based on gaining approval and praise from others and conforming to social norms.

Postconventional level: Moral decisions are based on a set of broad principles of justice that may transcend social laws and rules.

Preconventional level: Moral decisions are made based on a reward-punishment orientation.

Social contract orientation: Stage 5, postconventional level, in which an individual acknowledges that laws are important but must be questioned if individual rights are not upheld.

Universal ethical principle orientation: Stage 6, postconventional level, in which principles of right and wrong are based on universal justice and respect for the dignity of all humans, which may conflict with and transcend social law.

12 to 18
Adolescence – Social, Emotional,
And Moral Development
Moral Development

Name _____

Section _____

APPLICATION: KNOWLEDGE IN ACTION

1. Describe the responses of the adolescents in the video when presented with Kohlberg's Heinz dilemma. Are their responses typical for adolescents? Why or why not?

2. Discuss the developmental progression of moral reasoning according to Kohlberg. What level of moral reasoning do the responses of the adolescents in the video reflect? Are any of their responses based on a social contract or universal ethical principle orientation? Cite specific examples to support your answer.

12 to 18
Adolescence – Social, Emotional,
And Moral Development
Moral Development

Name _____

Section _____

3. As these adolescents move through adulthood, are they likely to continue to make moral decisions at their current level of moral reasoning? Why or why not?

CONNECTING CONTENT: RESEARCH AND THEORIES IN ACTION

Summary of Observation Module Content

- Interview 1: Alan, age 18.
- Group Interview with Teens.
- Interview 2: Jason, age 17.

Observation Module Questions	Name _____
12 to 18 Years	Section _____

1. How does Alan describe his relationship with his parents? How would you characterize his parents' parenting style? Discuss research findings on the effects of parenting on an adolescent's social, emotional, and academic development, using Alan as an example.

2. Do Alan's responses to interview questions endorse the theories of Erikson, Piaget, and Kohlberg? Why or why not? Cite specific examples to support your answer.

3. Parents are often concerned that negative peer pressure will influence their teenage child, leading him or her down the wrong path. All of the teens in the video discuss peer pressure, crowds, and conformity. How do they describe the effects of crowd affiliation, peer pressure, and conformity in their lives? Are their responses consistent with research? Why or why not?

4. Jason candidly discusses his views on sex, alcohol, and other choices faced by teens today. Describe his views on these topics. Is Jason a "typical" teenager? Why or why not?